Hulk Hogan

Pro Wrestler
Terry Bollea

by Angie Peterson Kaelberer

Reading Consultant:
Dr. Robert Miller
Professor of Special Education
Minnesota State University, Mankato

CAPSTONE
HIGH-INTEREST
BOOKS

an imprint of Capstone Press
Mankato, Minnesota

Capstone High-Interest Books are published by Capstone Press
151 Good Counsel Drive, P.O. Box 669, Mankato, Minnesota 56002
www.capstonepress.com

Printed in the United States of America in Stevens Point, Wisconsin.
112009
005632R

Library of Congress Cataloging-in-Publication Data
Kaelberer, Angie Peterson.
    Hulk Hogan: pro wrestler Terry Bollea / by Angie Peterson Kaelberer.
    p. cm.—(Pro wrestlers)
    Summary: Traces the life and career of the professional wrestler known as
Hulk Hogan.
    Includes bibliographical references (p. 45) and index.
    ISBN-13: 978-0-7368-2140-7 (hardcover)
    ISBN-10: 0-7368-2140-6 (hardcover)
    1. Hogan, Hulk, 1955—Juvenile literature. 2. Wrestlers—United States—
Biography—Juvenile literature. [1. Hogan, Hulk, 1955– 2. Wrestlers.] I. Title.
II. Series.
GV1196.H64 K34 2004
796.812'092—dc21
                    2002156119

Editorial Credits
Karen Risch, product planning editor; Timothy Halldin, series designer;
    Patrick Dentinger, book designer; Jo Miller, photo researcher

Photo Credits
Dr. Michael Lano, cover (main), 17, 18, 23, 28, 33, 34, 36, 39
Getty Images/Elsa Hasch, cover (right inset); Andy Lyons, 14; Will Hart, 20;
    Liaison/Arnaldo Magnani, 30; Liaison/Russell Turiak, 42
Michael Blair, cover (left inset), 10, 13, 24, 27, 40
Wire Image/George Pimentel, 4, 7

Capstone Press thanks Dr. Michael Lano, WReaLano@aol.com, for his assistance in the
preparation of this book.

Feb 2010

Table of Contents

Chapter 1

A Great Comeback

On March 17, 2002, more than 68,000 fans filled the SkyDome in Toronto, Ontario, Canada. The fans were there for the biggest event in pro wrestling, WrestleMania.

The fans cheered as Terry Bollea walked into the ring. Terry is known as Hulk Hogan. His opponent was Dwayne Johnson. Johnson wrestles as The Rock.

The match was an important one for Terry. He had wrestled for the World Wrestling Federation (WWF) from 1983 to 1993. In 1994, he joined World Championship Wrestling (WCW). Terry returned to the WWF in February 2002. He did not know if WWF fans still remembered or cared about him.

Terry wrestled The Rock at WrestleMania 18 in Toronto, Ontario.

Crowd Favorite

The fans cheered as Terry began the match by throwing The Rock to the mat. Terry and The Rock traded punches until Terry ran out of the ring. The Rock followed. He hit Terry on the head and rolled him back into the ring. By this time, nearly all of the fans were chanting, "Hogan, Hogan."

Later in the match, Terry hit The Rock in the head and shoved him into the referee. The referee fell to the mat. The Rock took Terry down with a spinebuster, but Terry got up. The Rock then took Terry down with a sharpshooter. The Rock grabbed Terry's leg and twisted it back. In pain, Terry tapped his hand on the mat. The referee was still down and did not see Terry tapping out. The Rock dropped Terry's leg and tried to wake up the referee.

An Exciting Finish

Terry then took The Rock down with The Rock's own signature move, the Rock Bottom. Terry stood next to The Rock as he wrapped his arms around The Rock's head and neck. He then slammed The Rock's body to the mat and covered him for the pin. The Rock kicked out.

Terry was the fans' favorite during his match against The Rock.

The Rock then used the Rock Bottom to take
Terry down, but Terry kicked out.

Terry kicked The Rock to the mat. Terry then
used his signature move, the leg drop. He ran
across the ring and kicked both legs in the air.
He put all of his weight on his legs as he landed
on The Rock. Terry then covered The Rock for
the pin, but The Rock kicked out. Terry kicked
The Rock to the mat again. He tried to land
another legdrop but missed.

> I realized that this [the match with The Rock] was the most important, unbelievable thing that's ever happened in my career.—Terry Bollea, WWE *Hulkamania* magazine, 2002

The Rock got to his feet. He took Terry down with a Rock Bottom. He then picked up Terry and did another Rock Bottom. The Rock followed this move with the People's Elbow. He speared Terry with his elbow as he fell on top of him. The referee counted to three. The Rock had defeated Terry.

Although he lost, Terry was happy. He had wrestled a great match against one of the WWF's top wrestlers.

About Hulk Hogan

Terry Bollea is 6 feet, 7 inches (201 centimeters) tall and weighs 275 pounds (125 kilograms). He began his wrestling career in 1977. Terry won five WWF World Championships and six WCW Championships. After the WWF bought WCW, these titles were combined into the WWF Undisputed Championship. Terry won this title in April 2002.

In 2002, Terry published his autobiography. This book about his life is called *Hollywood Hulk Hogan*.

Major Matches

January 23, 1984—Terry defeats the Iron Sheik to win his first WWF World Championship.

March 29, 1987—Terry pins Andre the Giant in front of more than 93,000 fans at WrestleMania 3.

April 2, 1989—Terry defeats "Macho Man" Randy Savage to win his second WWF World Championship.

March 24, 1991—Terry wins his third WWF World Championship by defeating Sergeant Slaughter.

April 4, 1993—Terry becomes the first five-time WWF World Champion by defeating Yokozuna.

July 17, 1994—Terry defeats Ric Flair to win his first WCW World Championship.

July 12, 1999—Terry wins his sixth WCW World Championship title by defeating Randy Savage.

March 17, 2002—Terry wrestles The Rock at WrestleMania 18.

April 21, 2002—Terry defeats Triple H to become the WWF Undisputed Champion.

Chapter 2

The Early Years

Terry Bollea was born August 11, 1953, in Augusta, Georgia. His father, Pete, worked for a construction company. His mother, Ruth, was a secretary. Terry had two older brothers, Kenneth and Allan. Soon after Terry was born, the family moved to Tampa, Florida.

Early Dreams

Terry was overweight as a child. By age 12, he weighed 200 pounds (91 kilograms). Terry liked to play sports, but his weight made him run slowly. But Terry had strong arms. He was a champion bowler and a good hitter in baseball.

Terry was born in Augusta, Georgia.

Terry also liked pro wrestling. A company called Florida Championship Wrestling put on shows in Tampa. Terry and his father went to these matches every week.

Besides sports, Terry was interested in music. He learned how to play guitar when he was in junior high. By ninth grade, Terry was in a rock band. Terry played in bands during his four years at Robinson High School.

A New Direction

In 1970, Terry graduated from high school. He started taking classes at St. Petersburg Junior College in St. Petersburg, Florida. He also played in a band at a local nightclub.

Terry was still overweight. He started working out in a gym. He lost weight and began developing his muscles.

Pro wrestlers also came to the gym. Terry became friends with some of the wrestlers. He started thinking about a career as a wrestler.

In 1972, Terry graduated from St. Petersburg Junior College. He started taking classes at the University of South Florida in Tampa.

Terry grew up watching Florida Championship Wrestling. His favorite wrestler was Dusty Rhodes. Rhodes was born in 1945. His real name is Virgil Runnels Jr. Rhodes started wrestling in 1969. He stood 6 feet, 1 inch (185 centimeters) tall and weighed about 300 pounds (136 kilograms) when he wrestled.

Early in his career, Rhodes wrestled for the American Wrestling Association (AWA) and the National Wrestling Alliance (NWA). He also wrestled as an independent in Florida. In 1979, he won the NWA World Heavyweight Championship three times. He later wrestled in the WWF and WCW. Later in his career, he set up matches and worked as an announcer. In 1995, he was named to the WCW Hall of Fame.

Terry dreamed of a career as a pro wrestler.

Training for a Dream

In 1976, Terry met pro wrestler Hiro Matsuda. Matsuda owned a gym where he trained other pro wrestlers. Terry went to work out with Matsuda. Terry broke his leg during his first day of training. Terry did not want to quit wrestling. After his leg healed, he returned to Matsuda's gym.

Terry decided to focus on his wrestling training. He dropped out of college and quit playing in the band. He got a job unloading ships at Tampa's docks. The job helped pay for his training.

Terry practiced with pro wrestlers. These men were tough on Terry in the ring. They wanted to make sure that he was serious about becoming a wrestler. Terry was in a great deal of pain from his training, but he did not quit. He wanted to succeed at wrestling.

Early Matches

Late in 1977, wrestling promoter Eddie Graham came to watch Terry wrestle. Graham thought Terry was ready for his first match. Terry's dream of being a pro wrestler was about to come true.

Terry wrestled his first match as the Super Destroyer. He wrestled Brian Blair. The two men wrestled for 20 minutes, but neither wrestler was able to pin the other. The match ended in a draw.

Terry started wrestling in Tampa. After four months, he was making only $25 each week. Terry decided to look for another job.

A Break from Wrestling

Terry took some time off from wrestling.
He moved to Cocoa Beach, Florida. Terry
managed a nightclub and a gym. He hired his
friend Ed Leslie to help him. Terry also began
teaching Ed how to wrestle.

In 1978, Terry and Ed started wrestling
as a tag team. They called themselves Terry
Boulder and Ed Boulder as they wrestled in
Florida and Alabama.

Becoming Hulk Hogan

While wrestling in Alabama, Terry got a new
wrestling name. He appeared on a TV talk
show with actor Lou Ferrigno. Ferrigno played
the Hulk on the TV show *The Incredible Hulk*.
The talk show's host said that Terry was bigger
than Ferrigno. Other wrestlers started calling
Terry "The Hulk."

Terry got more wrestling jobs as he became
more popular. He wrestled in Tennessee as
Terry "The Hulk" Boulder. In Georgia, he
wrestled as Sterling Golden.

In 1979, Terry met Vincent J. McMahon.
McMahon owned the World Wide Wrestling

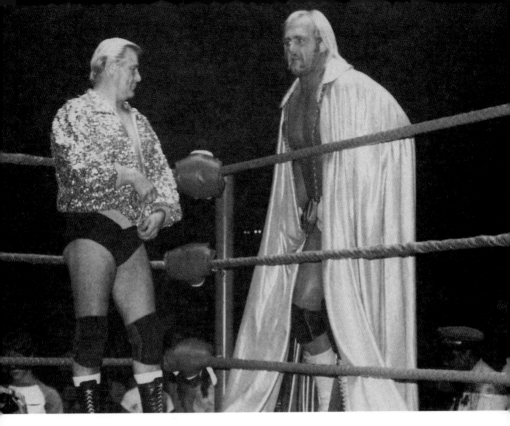

Pat Patterson was one of Terry's opponents during his first years in the WWF.

Federation (WWWF) in New York City.
Today, this wrestling company is called World
Wrestling Entertainment (WWE). McMahon
liked the way Terry looked and wrestled. Terry
joined the WWWF as Hulk Hogan.

Wrestlers play roles during their matches.
Some wrestlers are heroes. They are known as
"babyfaces." Other wrestlers are mean to their

In the AWA, Terry often wrestled Nick Bockwinkel.

opponents and the fans. These wrestlers are
called "heels." Terry was a heel when he joined
the WWWF. Fans often booed him. Terry did
not mind. He was finally making a living as a
pro wrestler.

In 1981, actor Sylvester Stallone called Terry. Stallone asked Terry to try out for a part in the movie *Rocky III*. Terry got the part. He asked Vincent McMahon for 10 days off to act in the movie. McMahon refused. Terry quit the WWWF and went to California to make the movie.

After Terry finished the movie, he went to Japan to wrestle. When he came back, he called promoter Verne Gagne. Gagne owned the American Wrestling Association (AWA) in Minneapolis, Minnesota. Terry joined the AWA as a heel, but the fans cheered for him. He became a babyface.

His part in *Rocky III* made Terry more popular. People who did not watch wrestling knew who he was. One day, Vincent K. McMahon called Terry. McMahon was Vincent J. McMahon's son. He had bought the WWWF from his father and renamed it the World Wrestling Federation (WWF). McMahon wanted Terry to wrestle for the WWF.

On December 18, 1983, Terry married Linda Claridge in Los Angeles. A few days later, Terry and Linda traveled to New York City. Terry was about to become a WWF superstar.

Chapter 3

Hulkamania

On January 23, 1984, Terry wrestled his first big match for the WWF. He faced Jose Azzeri at Madison Square Garden in New York City. Azzeri wrestled as the Iron Sheik. He was also the WWF World Champion.

Terry defeated the Iron Sheik with a legdrop in front of more than 20,000 fans. Terry was the new WWF World Champion. He would hold the title for more than four years.

Beginnings of Hulkamania

Terry quickly became the most popular wrestler in the WWF. He started calling his fans "Hulkamaniacs." He would ask his

Terry became the WWF World Champion in 1984.

opponents, "What are you going to do when Hulkamania runs wild all over you?"

Terry was especially popular with children. Terry would tell his young fans to train, say their prayers, and take their vitamins. He often visited sick children in hospitals and gave disabled children tickets to his matches.

WrestleMania

On March 29, 1987, Terry had one of the biggest matches of his career. He faced Andre Roussimoff at WrestleMania 3. Roussimoff was known as Andre the Giant.

Andre had wrestled for the WWF for 15 years. He weighed more than 500 pounds (227 kilograms). Andre had never lost a match by a pin. Terry wanted to be the first WWF wrestler to pin Andre.

WrestleMania 3 was held in the Pontiac Silverdome in Pontiac, Michigan. More than 93,000 fans filled the stands. This crowd was the largest ever for an indoor sports event.

Andre controlled most of the early action in the match. He punched Terry and kicked him in the face. Andre then kicked Terry out of the

Terry wrestled some of his greatest matches against Andre the Giant.

ring. Andre tried to headbutt Terry, but he hit his head on the ringpost instead. Andre then picked up Terry and backdropped him onto the concrete floor. Andre rolled Terry back into the ring. He lifted his leg up to kick Terry in the face. Terry ducked and clotheslined Andre into the ropes. He then used all of his strength to pick up Andre and slam him to the mat.

Terry fell on Andre with a legdrop as the referee counted to three. Terry was the first WWF wrestler to pin Andre the Giant.

More Championships

Terry held his title until February 5, 1988. That night, Andre the Giant defeated him. Terry then teamed with Randy Poffo to form the Mega-Powers tag team. Poffo wrestles as "Macho Man" Randy Savage.

By 1989, Savage was the WWF World Champion. Terry challenged him to a title match at WrestleMania 5 on April 2. Terry defeated Savage to win his second WWF World Championship.

Terry held the World Champion belt for almost a year. On April 1, 1990, he faced Jim Hellwig at WrestleMania 6 in Toronto, Canada. Hellwig wrestled as the Ultimate Warrior. He pinned Terry and took his World Champion title.

Terry was still wrestling well. On January 19, 1991, he defeated 29 other wrestlers to win

Terry was the WWF World Champion from April 1989 until April 1990.

the Royal Rumble in Miami, Florida. In March, he challenged WWF Champion Robert Remus to a match at WrestleMania 7. Remus wrestled as Sergeant Slaughter. Terry defeated Slaughter to win his third WWF World Championship belt.

On November 27, 1991, Terry lost his title again. Mark Callaway, who wrestles as the Undertaker, defeated him at Survivor Series. Terry won the title back from the Undertaker just six days later. Richard Fliehr, who wrestles as Ric Flair, interfered in the match and helped Terry win. The next day, WWF officials took the title away from Terry because of Flair's actions. No one held the title until Flair won the Royal Rumble on January 19, 1992.

By 1993, Bret Hart was the WWF World Champion. At WrestleMania 9, Rodney Anoia defeated Hart to win the title. Anoia wrestled as Yokozuna. Terry then challenged Yokozuna to another match. Terry defeated Yokozuna. He became the first wrestler to win the WWF World Championship five times.

Rival in the Ring: Andre the Giant

Andre Roussimoff was born in 1945 in France. At age 19, he began wrestling in France.

Andre had a rare disease that made his body keep growing during most of his life. Andre grew until he was 7 feet, 5 inches (226 centimeters) tall and weighed about 500 pounds (227 kilograms).

Andre joined the WWWF in 1972 as Andre the Giant. His size and personality made him popular with wrestling fans. In 1988, he defeated Terry to win the WWF World Championship. A year later, Andre teamed with Uliuli Fifita to win the WWF Tag Team Championship. Fifita wrestles as Haku.

Like Terry, Andre was an actor. He appeared in several TV shows and in the movie *The Princess Bride*.

Andre continued wrestling into the 1990s. He died of a heart attack in 1993.

In 1993, Terry acted in the movie *Mr. Nanny*.

A Break from the WWF

Winning his fifth title did not make Terry
happy. Terry had been injured many times.
He often was in pain when he wrestled. By
this time, Terry and Linda had two children,
Brooke and Nicholas. Terry missed spending
time with his family.

Terry's unhappiness started to show in the
ring. Fans began to boo him. Terry began to
think about leaving pro wrestling.

My attitude was horrible ... at the end of my run here, it was quite obvious that I wasn't a happy camper.—Terry Bollea, WWE *Hulkamania* magazine, 2002

On June 13, 1993, Terry lost his WWF World Championship to Yokozuna. He then left the WWF.

A New Career

Terry continued to act while he was with the WWF. He appeared on TV shows and in the movies *No Holds Barred, Suburban Commando,* and *Mr. Nanny.*

After he left the WWF, Terry thought about being a full-time actor. Terry was offered a part in a TV show called *Thunder in Paradise.* Terry worked for more than a year as an actor and producer on the show.

Thunder in Paradise was filmed at a studio in Orlando, Florida. World Championship Wrestling (WCW) filmed one of its wrestling shows at the same studio. One day, Ric Flair came to see Terry. Flair was now wrestling for WCW. Flair said WCW owner Ted Turner would like to hire Terry. After *Thunder in Paradise* went off the air, Terry thought about Turner's offer. In July 1994, he joined WCW.

Chapter 4

WCW Star

On July 17, 1994, Terry wrestled his first match in WCW. Terry faced Ric Flair for the WCW World Championship at Bash at the Beach in Orlando, Florida. Terry defeated Flair to win his first WCW title.

Terry held the WCW World Championship until October 29, 1995. That night, Paul Wight defeated Terry. At the time, Wight wrestled as the Giant. Today, he wrestles for WWE as the Big Show.

A New Direction

Terry had been a babyface during most of his career. He had joined WCW as a babyface.

Ric Flair was Terry's first opponent in WCW.

Terry wanted to take the Hulk Hogan character in a new direction.

On July 26, 1996, WCW wrestlers were in Daytona Beach, Florida, for Bash at the Beach. At the event, wrestlers Larry Pfohl and Steve Borden teamed with Randy Savage. Pfohl wrestled as Lex Luger, while Borden was Sting. Savage, Luger, and Sting faced Kevin Nash and Scott Hall. Nash and Hall were heels who had just left the WWF to join WCW.

Near the end of the match, Luger was injured. Hall and Nash teamed up against Savage in the ring. Terry then walked to the ring. The fans thought Terry would help Savage. Instead, Terry joined Nash and Hall to defeat Savage.

That night, Terry, Nash, and Hall formed a heel group called the New World Order (nWo). Terry changed his character's name to "Hollywood" Hulk Hogan. He stopped wearing red and yellow in the ring. Instead, he wore sunglasses, black jeans and T-shirt, and a black bandanna.

In 1996, Terry helped form the nWo.

The change in Terry's character shocked wrestling fans. But Nash, Hall, and Terry worked well together. The fans began to cheer for the nWo. More wrestlers joined the nWo. Soon, more people were watching WCW's TV shows than the WWF's TV shows.

On August 10, 1996, Terry defeated the Giant for the WCW World Championship. Terry held the title for nearly one year.

Terry often wrestled Sting during the late 1990s.

On August 4, 1997, Terry lost the title to
Lex Luger. Just five days later, Terry
defeated Luger to win his third WCW World
Championship. Terry held the title until
December 28, 1997, when he lost it to Sting.

The End of WCW

During the next two years, Terry won the
WCW World Championship three more times.

But his victories did not make him happy. The WWF's TV shows had become more popular than WCW's shows. Some WCW officials blamed Terry for WCW's loss in popularity. The officials thought Terry was too old to wrestle. Terry sometimes did not get to wrestle on TV for weeks at a time.

On July 9, 2000, Terry was scheduled to wrestle Jeff Jarrett for the WCW World Championship at Bash at the Beach in Daytona, Florida. When Jarrett got in the ring, he refused to wrestle Terry. Jarrett lay down in the ring and Terry pinned him.

The fans at Bash at the Beach were upset with the way Terry won the belt. They wanted Terry and Jarrett to wrestle. Terry walked out of the ring as the fans booed. WCW official Vince Russo then came to the ring. He said that Terry's match with Jarrett did not count. Jarrett was still the WCW World Champion. Russo also said that Terry would never wrestle for WCW again.

Eight months after Terry left WCW, the company was sold to Vince McMahon. World Championship Wrestling was finished.

Chapter 5

Hulk Hogan Today

After he left WCW, Terry took some time off. He spent time with his family. He also had an operation to fix his knee. Terry spent many months in physical therapy after his operation.

Another Opportunity

In September 2001, Terry's father, Pete, became sick. Pete told Terry that he did not like how Terry had ended his wrestling career. Pete said Terry should wrestle again.

Pete died on December 28, 2001. Terry was sad about his father's death, but he thought about Pete's words. He began to think about wrestling again.

In 2001, Terry began to think about returning to pro wrestling.

I can't believe that the Federation gave
me the opportunity to fulfill my dream
and complete this journey by becoming
the Undisputed Champion.
—Terry Bollea, WWF.com, 4/21/02

Vince McMahon called Terry after Pete died.
McMahon told Terry that Nash and Hall were
returning to the WWF. McMahon wanted Terry
to join Hall and Nash in a new version of the
nWo. Terry agreed to McMahon's offer.

A New Start

On February 17, 2002, the nWo members came
to No Way Out in Milwaukee, Wisconsin. They
were still heels, but the fans cheered for them.

At WrestleMania 18, Terry wrestled The Rock.
After The Rock defeated Terry, Terry turned on
Hall and Nash. He left the nWo and started
wearing red and yellow in the ring again.

A Champion Again

In April 2002, Terry got a chance to win another
WWF title. Terry challenged Paul Levesque
to a match for the Undisputed Championship.
Levesque wrestles as Triple H.

Triple H controlled most of the early action
in the match. Later, Terry came back to take
Triple H down with a legdrop. As Terry went for

Terry formed a new version of the nWo with X-Pac, Kevin Nash, and Scott Hall.

the pin, wrestler Chris Irvine ran up to the ring. Irvine wrestles as Chris Jericho. Jericho pulled the referee out of the ring. Jericho then hit Terry with a chair and rolled the referee back into the ring. Jericho ran into the ring. Triple H then clotheslined him over the top rope for interfering in the match.

Terry then tried to take down Triple H with a legdrop, but missed. Triple H then took Terry

In May 2002, the Undertaker challenged Terry to a match for the Undisputed Championship.

down with a Pedigree. Triple H held Terry face down between his legs. Triple H then dropped to his knees as he slammed Terry's head to the mat.

Triple H went to cover Terry for the pin. The Undertaker then ran into the ring. He punched the referee and hit Triple H with a chair. The Undertaker picked up Terry and dropped him on top of Triple H. Instead of going for the pin, Terry stood up. He clotheslined the Undertaker over the top rope. Terry then did a legdrop on Triple H. The referee counted to three. Terry was the WWF Undisputed Champion.

Terry held the Undisputed Championship for only one month. On May 19, 2002, the Undertaker defeated Terry for the title. Terry was not upset to lose the title so soon. He was happy to be wrestling again.

Beyond Wrestling

Terry and his family live in Clearwater, Florida. Terry enjoys spending time with his family when he is not working. He also likes to play the guitar and ride motorcycles.

Terry has had a longer career than most wrestlers. Many wrestlers retire before age 40. Terry knows that he cannot wrestle forever. He may continue wrestling part-time for WWE. He also may continue his acting career. Whatever Terry does in the future, wrestling fans will remember him as one of the greatest pro wrestlers ever.

Career Highlights

1953—Terry is born August 11 in Georgia.

1979—Terry joins the WWWF as Hulk Hogan.

1982—Terry acts in his first movie, *Rocky III*, and wrestles for the AWA.

1983—Terry joins the WWF.

1984—Terry wins his first WWF World Championship.

1991—Terry wins the Royal Rumble and his third and fourth WWF World Championships.

1993—Terry becomes the first five-time WWF World Champion.

1994—Terry joins WCW and wins his first WCW World Championship.

1999—Terry wins his sixth WCW World Championship.

2002—Terry becomes the WWF Undisputed Champion and publishes his autobiography.

Words to Know

autobiography (aw-toh-bye-OG-ruh-fee)—a book in which the author tells the story of his or her life

injury (IN-juh-ree)—damage or harm to the body

opponent (uh-POH-nuhnt)—a person who competes against another person

physical therapy (FIZ-uh-kuhl THER-uh-pee)—the treatment of diseased or injured muscles and joints by exercise, massage, and heat

referee (ref-uh-REE)—a person who makes sure athletes follow the rules of a sport

signature move (SIG-nuh-chur MOOV)—the move for which a wrestler is best known; this move also is called a finishing move.

undisputed (uhn-diss-PYOOT-ed)—something that is true

To Learn More

Alexander, Kyle. *Pro Wrestling's Most Punishing Finishing Moves*. Pro Wrestling Legends. Philadelphia: Chelsea House, 2001.

Burgan, Michael. *The Rock: Pro Wrestler Rocky Maivia*. Pro Wrestlers. Mankato, Minn.: Capstone Press, 2002.

Hunter, Matt. *The Story of the Wrestler They Call "Hollywood" Hulk Hogan*. Pro Wrestling Legends. Philadelphia: Chelsea House, 2000.

Kaelberer, Angie Peterson. *The Nature Boy: Pro Wrestler Ric Flair.* Pro Wrestlers. Mankato, Minn.: Capstone Press, 2004.

Useful Addresses

Professional Wrestling Hall of Fame
P.O. Box 434
Latham, NY 12110

World Wrestling Entertainment Inc.
1241 East Main Street
Stamford, CT 06902

Internet Sites

Do you want to learn more about Hulk Hogan?
Visit the FactHound at *http://www.facthound.com*

FactHound can track down many sites to help you. All
the FactHound sites are hand-selected by our editors.
FactHound will fetch the best, most accurate information
to answer your questions.

IT'S EASY! IT'S FUN!
1) Go to *http://www.facthound.com*
2) Type in: 0736821406
3) Click on "FETCH IT" and FactHound will put you on
   the trail of several helpful links.

You can also search by subject or book title. So, relax
and let our pal FactHound do the research for you!

Index